FUNERAL WARS

FUNERAL WARS

JONATHAN HARR

✳ SHORT BOOKS

FRONT LINES

First published in 2001 by
Short Books
15 Highbury Terrace
London N5 1UP

A CIP catalogue record for this book
is available from the British Library.

ISBN 0 571 20850 9

Printed in Great Britain by
Bookmarque Ltd, Croydon, Surrey

IN THE DEEP SOUTH of America, where racism still boils just beneath the surface of nearly all social interactions, a civil trial began one September morning in 1995 in the Hinds County circuit court in Jackson, Mississippi. Like most lawsuits, especially those that fail to settle before trial, this case had a long and complicated history and antagonists who had become bitter enemies.

It was, on the face of it, merely a contract dispute, similar to thousands that are filed in courts across the land each year, and in this respect it was unremarkable. Its outcome, however, caused consternation in circles far removed from Mississippi. This was in part because of revelations that emerged during the trial about the nature of a hugely profitable industry; one which sooner or later enters the life of every human being. Its dramatic impact was also the consequence of the involvement of an unusual legal advocate.

The Lawyer

Willie Edward Gary graduated from North Carolina Central University law school in June 1974. He was 26 years old, married with two sons, aged four and 11 months. On 1 July, he and his wife, Gloria, packed up their belongings and left their apartment in Raleigh and drove for 16 hours to Stuart, Florida.

He pulled up at the Raintree Run Apartments around mid-morning and went into the manager's office to pick up the key to a two-bedroom apartment that he had rented in a series of transactions by telephone and through the mail.

In Gary's recollection, the woman seated behind the desk looked at him curiously and asked him to wait a moment. She got up and went into another office, shutting the door behind her. When she returned, she said, 'I'm sorry, we don't have any vacant apartments.'

Gary showed the woman the receipt for the deposit he had sent. He showed her the correspondence he had received – paperwork concerning all the terms of the tenancy, even down to the use of the swimming pool. The woman said, 'I'm very sorry, but we just don't have any units available now.'

Gary said to the woman, 'I talked to you about hooking up the gas and electricity. Don't you remember that?

And now you're telling me you don't have an apartment?'

From the back office, a man emerged. Gary explained the circumstances again. 'My wife and two young children are outside in the car,' he said. 'We've got no place to go.' The man replied, 'I'm sorry, sir. We don't have an apartment.'

Gary said, 'You can keep me out. That's OK. But I want you to know that I just graduated from law school, and I'm going to sue you to kingdom come. I contracted with you, and it's clear that you don't want me here because my face is black.'

Gary turned and walked out to the car, where his wife and sons were waiting for him. He stood by the car, taut with anger, explaining the circumstances to his wife. As they debated what to do next, the man appeared at the door and called out his name. Within an hour, Gary had the keys to the apartment. He and his family were the first black people to live in the Raintree Run Apartments.

***

Willie Gary long ago departed the Raintree Run, but he finds himself on occasion driving by the apartment complex. He currently owns a blue Bentley, one of two that he bought recently to add to the several Mercedes-Benz he has already. Mercedes-Benz are commonplace in the affluent and mostly white enclave of Stuart, and Gary prefers that people take notice of his presence.

Being noticed serves him both personally and professionally: he makes his living as a personal-injury lawyer, and many personal-injury lawyers tend to advertise their success to potential clients by the cars they drive, the clothes they wear and the heavily jewelled watches that adorn their wrists. Gary wears $3,000 suits and a diamond-encrusted Rolex. He has cases pending in 42 states. He travels in his own plane: a Gulfstream II executive jet that he has named Wings of Justice. He has two offices in Florida, one in Stuart, the other in Fort Pierce. The larger of the two, in Stuart, occupies the former Pelican Hotel, a grand hacienda-style edifice that overlooks the Saint Lucie river. He has smaller offices in Texas, Mississippi and Louisiana. Twenty-seven lawyers work for him, along with a staff of 112 para-legals, secretaries, receptionists, accountants, stenographers, clerks, messengers, janitors, grounds-keepers, four private detectives, three pilots and an aviation mechanic. Because many of his cases concern claims of medical malpractice, he also employs five nurses and a doctor.

Gary stands just five feet seven inches tall, is thickly built across the shoulders, stout in the torso and well muscled in all his limbs. He walks with a distinctly pigeon-toed gait. His skin, which has a rich, dark-brown sheen, radiates health. He has a deep and resonant voice that carries well in courtrooms and from pulpits. Now aged 52, he wears his hair cropped close to his scalp, although as a young man he wore it variously in an Afro and a flat-top – a three-inch-high topiary of a flat-top, according to those who knew him back then – so that he would appear taller.

He arrived at college, at Shaw University in Raleigh, unbidden and without an application on file, in the hope of winning a football scholarship. He was sporting the flat-top and wearing platform shoes. But still the football players all called him 'Shorty'.

It was not vanity or lack of confidence that caused Gary to add extra height. He has rarely, it seems, suffered from a lack of confidence. The story of his life, which he has told on many occasions, with various embellishments and abridgements, with and without conscious exaggeration, has acquired, in its repetition, the contours of legend. Some facts, however, are verifiable.

The sixth of 11 children, Willie was born a twin on 12 July 1947, on a farm near Eastman, Georgia, to Mary and Turner Gary. His birth was, by all accounts, a difficult one. His twin did not survive, and he and his mother required hospitalisation. The medical bills forced Turner Gary to sell his farm and move his family to the town of Canal Point, Florida, on the shores of Lake Okeechobee. Willie spent much of his early childhood in a whitewashed three-room shack with a tar-paper roof and no electricity or plumbing. The shack was still standing a few years ago, in a state of advanced decay, overgrown with vines and palmetto trees.

Turner Gary had only a second-grade education. He supported his family by working in the cane fields and, later, when the family moved north to Indiantown, in the bean fields. In June, he would nail shut the windows and doors of the shack and take his family to the summer camps for migrant workers in the Carolinas. They would return in November, after the apple harvest, just as the winter crops were coming ripe in Florida. When the Gary children grew old enough to work, they joined their father and siblings in the fields. Willie began in 1952, aged five, carrying water and food to his family and the other workers in the fields.

Turner Gary had an enterprising mind. By the mid-1950s, he had acquired an old delivery truck, cut a panel out of the side, and fitted it out with a gas cooker. He made sandwiches and soups and carried cold drinks in a cooler, which he sold to the field-workers at lunch. Willie served as his chief assistant.

By the time Willie was ten, he was an experienced picker of sweetcorn, string beans, celery, cabbage and apples. Like other migrant children in the Carolinas, he went to school for half a day, in the morning. At noon, a bus would pick them up from school and take them directly to the fields. Back in Florida, Willie attended school for a full day, except during the height of the various picking seasons, when he would frequently miss a day or two each week to work in the fields.

The year that Willie Gary entered high school, in 1961, he returned to Florida in early September rather than in November so that he could try out for the football team. He made the team as a linebacker. The following year, his mother stopped travelling north to the fields and stayed at home with the youngest children; by 1964 his father had also quit the migrant trail. The family now made enough money in Florida, working in the cabbage fields and cornfields, and also by growing their own crops on a small plot of land.

While he was at high school, Willie started a lawn-mowing and yard-cleaning service aimed at the families of Indiantown. He talked the owner of Stuart Feed Supply into allowing him to buy a lawnmower on credit. He made his lawnmower payments faithfully. 'I paid every dime on time. My daddy always told me, "Pay your bills on time. Even if you can't eat, pay your bills, or explain why you can't."' He negotiated a deal for a second lawnmower and hired high-school friends to cut grass while he contracted with clients.

Willie Gary was not an exceptional student. He was, however, an energetic football player. He overcame his modest physical skills and diminutive size by application of energy and a will to succeed. In his senior year, he made the Treasure Coast Conference team and won an invitation to try out for a football scholarship at Bethune-Cookman, a small college for black students in Daytona. By his own account, he was the first boy from Indiantown to go off to college, and his departure was cause for celebration.

He arrived at Bethune-Cookman in August for three weeks of training camp. The coach, Jack McClairen, had played professionally for the Pittsburgh Steelers. At the end of each day's practice, Coach McClairen would call out the names of those boys who had failed to make the cut. Back then, in 1966, failing to make the cut meant failing to get the scholarship. On the last day of the training camp, a Friday in early September, McClairen summoned Gary to his office.

McClairen still remembers Willie Gary today. 'He was a small youngster, a marginal athlete. He didn't fit into what we needed at that time.' And McClairen told this to Gary, who broke down in tears. He pleaded that he would mow the field, clean the locker room, and wash uniforms if he could keep the scholarship. McClairen has no specific recollection of this moment, but he does not doubt Gary's account.

'A lot of my students would say, "This is the only way

for me to get an education. I'm the first in my family to go to college.' They'd just break down and start crying.. It was the most difficult part of my duties. It made you feel like a dog.'

Gary returned to Indiantown by bus that Friday night. The next morning, he called his high-school coach, Lewis Rice, and told him what had happened. Rice said to Willie Gary, 'You got discriminated against because you're a little guy. Jack McClairen don't like little guys.' Rice said he would call Dennis Jefferson, coach at Shaw University, in Raleigh, on Monday morning. He knew Jefferson personally. 'He's a small guy, used to be a quarterback,' Rice said.

On Sunday morning, Gary told his mother he was leaving for Raleigh that day. He and his girlfriend, Gloria Royal, packed his suitcase. He caught a Greyhound bus by the side of the road, arriving in Raleigh at dawn on Monday with $13 in his pocket. He walked two miles to Shaw University, and asked for directions to Coach Jefferson's office. He stood outside the coach's door for what seemed a long time, waiting for an audience. 'Those coaches', he now says, 'were mean just for nothing.' Finally, the coach asked him what he wanted.

'I'm here to try out for a scholarship,' he said. 'Coach Lewis Rice called about me.'

Jefferson said, 'I haven't had a call about you. We've

got a hundred players here trying out. You don't even have an application on file. You've got to go home.'

Gary told the coach that he didn't have enough money to get back home, and so Jefferson advised him to call home and get the money. 'We just can't have you here. I can't be responsible for you.'

Gary went directly to the admissions office, where he filled out an application. The dean of admissions, Dr Fleming, waived the $10 application fee but told him he would need a copy of his high-school report. Gary put in a collect-call to his high school. The secretary, Mrs Dixon, accepted the call. 'I'll never forget that lady for doing that,' says Gary. Mrs Dixon put a copy of the report in the mail that day.

Gary found his way to Tupper Memorial Hall, the football players' dormitory, where he met Jimmie Young, who today teaches high school in Chapel Hill, North Carolina, and Walter Johnson, from Melbourne, Florida. That evening, they brought him food from the cafeteria. He slept on a sofa in the dorm lounge.

Early the next morning, he went back to the gym and began cleaning up the locker room. Years later, in middle age, he would become fond of recalling his father's many maxims for negotiating one's way through life: 'My Daddy always said, "If you want a job, start working for nothing. They'll end up paying you." I guess it doesn't take a genius to figure that out, but a whole lot of people haven't figured it out yet.'

On Wednesday morning, the assistant coach came upon Gary cleaning up the locker room. He asked him who he was and what he was doing in the locker room. The boy told him his story. The assistant coach said, 'Man, you really want to go to school, don't you?'

Walking across the campus that afternoon, Gary encountered Coach Jefferson, whom he had been diligently trying to avoid. The coach asked if he'd got the money to go home. Gary said he was still waiting for it. Jefferson gave him a meal card that was good until Friday, and told him, 'By then, you better have your money. Meanwhile, help the trainer carry the stuff out to the football field.'

At the practice session on Friday afternoon, Gary was standing on the sidelines, watching the scrimmage, when one of the players was hurt. The coach told Gary, 'Baby, it's time to see what you can do.' Gary put on pads, a helmet and a jersey several sizes too big for him, and went on to the field. He recalls that on the first play he penetrated the offensive line, evading a trio of guards to reach the quarterback. He blocked two punts that afternoon.

Gary went on to make the Shaw University football team and received a scholarship. From the beginning, it was his habit to lead the players in prayer and in the team's fight songs. In his junior year, his team-mates elected him captain.

During his first year at college, he took remedial courses – as did most of the football players – and decided to major in business administration. In August, before the start of his second year, he married Gloria Royal, his girlfriend from Indiantown. She was the seventh of 11 children. Her father and Turner Gary had trucked together on the migrant route to the Carolinas. Gloria's first memory of Willie is of a summer day when, aged five, she and her older sister came across him changing the diaper of his brother Freddie and laughed at him. His first vivid memory of her is from second grade, when he was elected, along with Diane Jones and John Henry Rivers, to deliver a fruit basket to her at home, the custom in Indiantown when someone missed school because of illness. During his first year at Shaw, he had received as many as four letters a day from her.

The couple moved into a small apartment near the campus. Gloria, who had attended a junior college in Florida and was a diligent student, enrolled at Shaw and tutored her husband and the other football players. To make ends meet, Gary waited on tables and worked as a short-order cook. Then he began another landscaping business, renting equipment and hiring his team-mates as labourers. He called his business Gary's Home

Beautification Service and advertised in the quick-reference section of the local Raleigh paper. By his third year of college, with more business than he could handle, he hired a manager. He made enough money to buy a new Camaro, with an eight-track stereo. Coming upon a billboard announcing the construction of a 500-home trailer park, he went to the builder, an Orlando construction company, and offered his services as a landscaper. He said that he would clear rocks, seed grass and plant shrubbery for $175 per trailer home. Then he subcontracted the job out for $75 per yard. He cleared a profit on the job worth $50,000. His team-mates called him 'Little Boss Man'. One of them, Jimmie Young, recalls, 'We ragged him, but he was doing stuff you wouldn't believe. He was making more money than the college professors.'

Gary was subsequently accepted at North Carolina Central University law school in Durham. In his first year, he got one A, several Cs and a D, in criminal law. He knew he was no scholar. Without his football team-mates around him, he felt, he said, like 'the country bumpkin', but he sat in the front row of every class and applied himself to his studies more strenuously than he ever had at Shaw. Once, in a law-school exercise, he gave a closing argument in a case that concerned minor damages arising from a hypothetical car collision. The first words out of his mouth were: 'Members of the jury, I'm going to ask you for $1 million.' The other students gasped, and then laughed. Undeterred, he said, 'Why do I ask you for $1 million? Because the Constitution says I can.'

Gary felt no self-consciousness talking in front of an audience. 'I was used to standing in front of people in church, praying and singing.' He missed only two classes in three years of law school; and yet he also kept his landscaping business going to pay his tuition fees and to support his wife and children.

When Willie and Gloria moved back to Florida, to the Raintree Run Apartments in Stuart, he set himself the challenge of studying for the bar exam. He had heard that 97 per cent of black law-school graduates who took the Florida bar exam – a two-day ordeal – failed on their first attempt, and that most failed on their second, third and fourth attempts. He knew stories of black law-school students who had graduated *cum laude* failing repeatedly.

He studied for 18 hours a day. In October, after lengthy prayer with Gloria, he went to Jacksonville to take the exam. He left feeling that he'd genuinely done well.

While awaiting his result, he began looking in earnest for a job as a clerk or legal assistant. Lacking an introduction, he went from door to door to each local law firm in turn. All of them were run by white lawyers and usually Gary did not make it any further than the receptionist's desk. Finally, he found his way to the office of the Public Defender in Stuart, where Elton Schwarz, the director granted him an interview.

Schwarz was impressed by Gary. 'He had a drive to succeed. I knew his parents couldn't have financed an education. He had to have worked his way through law school.'

He told Gary that he had no money in the budget to hire a new lawyer, even though he needed one. His office covered a four-county area, and he had only four lawyers. 'If I had the money, I'd give you a job,' Schwarz said.

Gary said he would work for nothing. Schwarz, astonished by this offer, managed to come up with $25 a week in token pay, and told him, 'If I get additional funding, you can have a job.'

In his first week, Willie Gary accompanied Schwarz to the Saint Lucie county jail, where a man named Levis Leon Aldridge was awaiting trial for first-degree murder. Aldridge was accused of killing the manager of a local restaurant, where he had once worked as a dishwasher, in the course of a hold-up. Aldridge, who was white, had grown up in a tar-paper shack in Missouri and picked cotton. He had no previous history of violent crime, but now he faced the death penalty. When he saw Gary, Aldridge said to Schwarz, 'Who's the kid?'

Schwarz introduced them.

'You a lawyer?' Aldridge asked.

'No, sir,' said Gary, 'but I'm going to be one.'

For reasons that neither Schwarz nor Gary ever fathomed, Aldridge took a liking to Gary. 'It was very unusual,' Schwarz recalled. Just before Aldridge's second appearance before the judge, Schwarz told Gary, 'Leon wants you there.'

'What do I say in the courtroom?' Gary asked.

'Nothing,' said Schwarz. 'Leon just wants you there.'

In the courtroom, Aldridge was brought out in manacles and chains. The judge asked if the defendant was prepared to enter a plea. Schwarz stood up. 'My client wants –'

Aldridge brought both manacled fists down on the table. 'I want Willie Gary to represent me,' he said.

Gary, of course, had not yet passed the bar and thus could not address the court on behalf of Aldridge. But as they left the courtroom that day Schwarz said to him, 'You just hitched on to your first murder-one case.'

Some weeks later, on 20 November – Willie Gary recalls the date precisely – Schwarz stopped at the cubbyhole where Willie Gary worked. 'The results of the bar exam come out today,' Schwarz said. 'Do you want me to call and get your score?'

'No way,' Gary replied. 'If I'm going to get hurt, I want to open that envelope real slow.'

Schwarz went into his office and called for the bar-exam results anyway. He returned to Gary and said, 'I called them, Willie. You passed.'

Gary tried to reach Gloria at work, in Belle Glade, but she'd already left for home. He got in his car and drove towards Belle Glade, hoping to meet her on the highway. When he saw her car, he flagged her down and shouted from his window, 'Baby, I passed, I passed!' By the side of the road, they hugged and cried.

Willie Gary's formal admission to the Florida bar, on 20 December 1974, was cause for celebration in Indian-town. He was regarded by many of the townsfolk with an awe that bordered on reverence. When he came home to visit his parents, he would sit on the sofa in the living-room and a crowd would gather round and hang on every word he uttered. In the way that people customarily addressed a medical doctor, the people of Indiantown addressed him as 'Lawyer Gary'.

**

The capital-murder trial of Levis Leon Aldridge began on 6 January 1975. Elton Schwarz, who had just weeks earlier completed another capital-murder case, begged for an adjournment on the grounds that defence counsel was unprepared. The judge rejected the plea, and the trial went forward. It lasted for only three days. Aldridge maintained his innocence throughout, but the evidence against him was compelling.

Elton Schwarz conducted the examinations of the witnesses, but he did not feel sanguine about the outcome. Aldridge had wanted Gary to address the jury on his behalf, and Schwarz, who would speak last to the jury, agreed. Gary recalls that Schwarz said to him, 'You got Leon to listen to you. I know you can get the jury to listen.'

So it was that a freshly minted lawyer, a member of the bar for only three weeks, addressed the jury in the first real case of his life, a capital-murder trial. In Gary's memory, his plea to the jury was 'one hell of a closing argument' that kept the jurors 'deliberating for hours and hours'. In truth, the transcript reveals only a competent, workman-like argument. It was brief – Gary had only 30 minutes allotted to him – but not unskilful in its dissection of the credibility of the prosecution's two main witnesses. And the jurors did deliberate for two hours, although that is not very long in a death-penalty case. When Willie Gary recounted this tale of his first trial, he omitted the crucial part, leaving the listener to ask, 'So what happened to Aldridge?'

'He's on Death Row,' Willie Gary replied. 'If he hasn't been executed yet.'

Aldridge has not been executed, and he is no longer on Death Row. Also omitted from Gary's telling is Aldridge's appeal, on the grounds that his lawyers had provided ineffective counsel; that a mere legal intern – Gary – had prepared his case-in-chief. To save Aldridge from the death penalty, both Willie Gary and Elton Schwarz testified on his behalf, asserting that they had expected the judge to grant a 30-day continuance, and that they had indeed been unprepared for trial. Aldridge's appeal, rejected by the Florida Supreme Court, finally resulted in a retrial and a life sentence.

The day after the trial, Elton Schwarz called Gary into his office. The budget for the Public Defender's office, he said, had been reduced rather than increased, and he could not offer Gary a job.

Gary decided to start his own law firm. He and Gloria, with their life-savings of $1,500, began looking for an office in Stuart. They found a storefront on Colorado Avenue. It had a soiled pink carpet and grimy walls in need of paint. Together, they spent a week scrubbing the place. The other occupants of the shopping strip objected to Gary's presence. They thought his law office would attract vagrants and criminals.

Gary opened his door for business on 17 January. His first client was a woman named Bessie Lewis, who wanted to deed some property to one of her daughters. It was a simple matter for which Gary, on the advice of another lawyer in town, charged $400. But afterwards his conscience ate at him. He tried to return some of Bessie Lewis's money, but she refused it. He committed himself to representing her free for the rest of her life. That, too, proved to be a mistake, of another kind. When Bessie Lewis was overcharged $3 on her electricity bill, she called on Lawyer Gary to rectify matters. When her Sears washing machine broke down, it was Lawyer Gary who examined the warranty and set matters straight.

In his first year of business, Gary dealt with small matters criminal and domestic. In his second year, he represented the widow of a truck driver who had died in an accident in Palatka, Florida, near the Georgia border. The court records have been destroyed, but the case is still vivid in Gary's memory. The truck driver, Charlie Hayes, who was black, had swerved to avoid crushing the car of an elderly white lady, Mrs Ella Dancy, who had gone through a stop sign. Charlie Hayes's truck went off the road and into a barn, where Hayes was decapitated by falling timber.

Palatka is in Putnam County, which has a long and ugly history of Ku-Klux Klan activity. Gary figured that he needed to settle the case. He asked for $35,000. The insurance-company lawyer who represented Ella Dancy offered $20,000. The case was put on the trial calendar. Having read in books on trial practice that a lawyer should get to know his client, Gary took a bus to North Carolina to visit Charlie Hayes's widow. On a rainy afternoon, they sat on the front porch together, overlooking a small plot of land that Charlie Hayes had farmed. It was choked with weeds. There was a leak in the roof, under which Mrs Hayes had put a bucket.

'If Charlie was here, he'd fix it,' Mrs Hayes told him.

Gary presented the case before an all-white jury. He survived the routine defence motion asking the judge to dismiss the case on the grounds that the evidence was insufficient. In the closing argument, he recalls saying to the jurors, 'I was told that Mrs Hayes couldn't get a fair trial in this county. Maybe I'm naive, but when you raised your hand and swore you'd render a fair verdict I believed in you.'

And then he described the day he'd spent with Mrs Hayes. 'I can tell you about the grass in the field that hasn't been mowed, and the leak in the roof that hasn't been fixed, because Charlie's not around to take care of these things. But I can't tell you what Mrs Hayes feels. The only thing I can tell you is that when I was sitting with her on the front porch she heard a truck blow its horn out in the distance. She said, "Lawyer Gary, that's my Charlie now. He's coming home." I said to her, "No, that's not Charlie. He's not coming home again."' In his telling, it was at this point that he saw a woman on the jury take a handkerchief from her purse and dab her eyes.

'Don't give us charity,' he recalls saying to the jurors. 'Just do what's right.' He suggested that $225,000 was about right in this instance. When the jury returned its verdict, it was, he says, 'to the penny' what he had asked for.

The case helped to establish Gary's reputation locally, and it also established in his mind a desire to concentrate his practice on personal-injury law. He began getting referrals from other lawyers. His business grew. He moved to a larger office and took on a partner, and then another. For a time, he aimed at building the biggest black law firm in the nation, even though, as it turned out, he had more white clients than black. In a contract case, he sought the help of a retired white lawyer, a former city and school-board attorney from Michigan, who had come to Florida to fish and sail. They formed a friendship, and they prevailed in the contract case. Two weeks later, Gary invited this lawyer, whose name was Robert Parenti, to join his firm. Parenti, on brief consideration, decided that working with Gary might prove more fun than full-time fishing and sailing.

In his second year as a lawyer, Gary negotiated his first million-dollar settlement. In the years that followed, he asked juries on many occasions for million-dollar verdicts, but he did not win his first million-dollar jury verdict – the trial lawyer's benchmark of success – until 1984. The next year, in a case against Florida Power & Light involving the electrocution deaths of seven family members, he negotiated a settlement of more than $40 million. After that, big cases seemed to arrive almost routinely at his office.

Gary's office keeps a roster of his biggest cases and their awards. Against a Florida hospital, in the misdiagnosis of a seven-month-old girl with meningitis, and the alleged alteration of medical records: $17.7 million. Against an Atlanta hospital, in a circumcision procedure that severely burnt the penis of a one-day-old boy: $22.8 million. Against an osteopath and the Chicago Board of Education, in the paralysis of a high-school football player: $3.95 million. Against a Coca-Cola bottler, in the brain-damage of a two-year-old boy hit by a company van: $8 million. By 1996, Willie Gary had accumulated nearly 60 settlements or verdicts of $1 million or more.

Nowadays, the lawyers and investigators on his staff prepare most cases. The firm's monthly calendar of work lists, on average, 30 cases in various stages of mediation, settlement and trial. In December 1996, for example, the calendar contained cases in Ohio, Georgia, Mississippi, Virginia, North Carolina and Florida. As a rule, Gary becomes personally involved when a case is ready for trial or settlement. The vast majority of all civil claims settle before trial, but he usually goes to trial on as many as seven cases in a year.

During trial, Gary begins his mornings by listening to gospel music at a volume just short of deafening. As he dresses, he sings along to the Mighty Clouds of Joy or the Gospel Warriors, pausing occasionally to shadow-box. He wears hand-tailored shirts and gold cuff links, but he does not wear his bejewelled Rolex in front of jurors. Before heading off to the courtroom, he gathers his trial team – the lawyers, the expert witnesses, the secretaries, the clients – in a circle, and all hold hands as he prays for divine guidance and victory. Like many trial lawyers, he has superstitions. Walking to the courthouse, no member of the team may cross to the other side of the street, or deviate around a lamppost, or ascend a flight of stairs on the opposite side of a railing. He keeps an eagle eye out for infractions, and if he spies one the offender must retrace his steps.

He begins every trial by telling jurors that he would like to keep things simple. 'I'm just a country boy,' he says. 'If I just talk in plain ordinary talk about what happened, you won't hold that against me, will you?' Eloquence in the classic oratorical sense holds little appeal for him. His presentation is sometimes repetitive, occasionally erratic. His verb tenses often do not match. Sometimes he omits verbs altogether. He uses double negatives. He refers in openings and closings to at least one of his father's homilies, of which he has an apparently inexhaustible supply. He lapses now and then, when it suits his purpose, into the cadences of the pulpit. His voice fills a courtroom. His presence fills the courtroom, too. A white lawyer whose case he once took over at the behest of the client, and who was therefore not particularly well-disposed towards him, said about him, 'He acts like he's the most important guy in the world. The thing is he makes everybody else around him feel important, too. That's his genius.'

Gary has never smoked, and he does not drink alcohol – in his entire life, he can recall only once having had a sip of champagne. He has given large sums of money to religious, educational and charitable institutions. In 1991, for example, he pledged $10 million to Shaw University, which was then close to bankruptcy, and led a drive that raised another $17 million. His great indulgence is lavish spending, and in this he can match the excesses of any corporate mandarin. The interior of his Gulfstream jet, for example, is outfitted with 18k gold fixtures. The newest of his two homes, a Mediterranean-style villa on the Saint Lucie River at Sewall's Point, has some 40 rooms and 12 bathrooms, a gym and a movie theatre. He employs three full-time staff to care for the house, although Gloria, at her own insistence, continues to cook the meals. The family eats in the kitchen.

The Defendant

Like Willie Gary, Ray Loewen comes from a large family. He was born in 1940, the tenth of 12 children of parents of Mennonite background, in the small rural community of Steinbach, in the province of Manitoba, Canada. He, too, eventually became rich.

His father ran the town's only funeral parlour and ambulance service. The Loewen family, which occupied a large house adjacent to the funeral parlour, always struggled to make ends meet. From an early age, Ray assisted his father in the family business. By the time he was 13, he was driving the station wagon that served as an ambulance. He and his father covered most of south-east Manitoba, appearing at the scene of all local tragedies – murders, suicides and car accidents – to recover bodies. In his memory, many of these journeys seemed to occur late on winter nights. He learnt from his father how to embalm and prepare a corpse for burial, and how to lift a casket containing a body and liner-box – 400 or more pounds – into the funeral wagon.

Despite this early training, Ray had little idea what he wanted to do in life. His father, who regarded the funeral business as a ministry of sorts, urged him to enter theological college. Lacking a direction of his own, Ray did so, but he soon realised that the 'calling', as he put it, 'was not very strong'. He returned home to help his father, who was by then ailing.

Ray Loewen's particular genius in life, as it emerged, did not lie in funeral-directing, but it found its first expression there, in managing the family business. The funeral home received, in an average year, 125 'calls' (as they are known in the trade), and took in around $25,000 dollars, about $240 per funeral. Loewen straightened out the accounts, raised prices to levels comparable with those of funeral homes in Winnipeg, and modernised the equipment and facilities. Within a few years, he had managed to put the funeral home on a firm financial footing. Then, in 1967, he bought another funeral home, in Fort Frances, Ontario. Two years later, over breakfast with a group of businessmen at the Rainy River Hotel, in Fort Frances, he heard that the owner of the second-largest funeral home – 400 calls a year – in New Westminster, near Vancouver, was looking for a buyer. Loewen had enough cash for only a small down-payment, but he successfully negotiated a graduated payment plan and acquired the funeral home for $447,000.

Even before making that purchase, Loewen had begun to think about the possibility of building a company comprising many funeral homes. He was an ambitious man and a gifted entrepreneur, but the idea that took shape in his mind back then, bold as it might have seemed to him, does not begin to compare with what the future held for him.

The funeral industry in the United States, as in Canada, was embarking on a period of evolutionary change after almost a century of stability. Before the Civil War, the care of the dead was the domain of the deceased's family and neighbours. The corpse was customarily laid out on a board that was draped with a sheet and supported by chairs at either end. The body was washed, almost always by a female member of the household, and wrapped in a sheet for burial. A local carpenter or furniture dealer supplied the coffin, a simple wooden box with a lid, and an undertaker – often the same carpenter or furniture dealer, or perhaps the owner of a livery stable – brought the coffin to the house and placed the body inside. With family and friends gathered around, a minister performed the appropriate religious rituals, and then the undertaker conveyed the coffin to the cemetery.

Funerals had been conducted in this manner for centuries. At about the time of the Civil War, however, embalming became more common in order to preserve the corpses of dead soldiers whose families wanted them shipped home. Embalming was not then a new or mysterious art – its practice, after all, dated back millennia, to ancient Egypt – but the Puritan ethos of early America regarded it as distasteful and unnatural. This sentiment changed greatly when the effects of embalming were witnessed by the huge audience that gathered in 1865 along the train route of Lincoln's funeral procession, which began in Washington, DC and ended in Springfield, Illinois.

Lincoln's corpse, of course, had had to be embalmed before making the long, slow journey. And it was not placed in a simple, rough-hewn coffin. His body was displayed in an ornate mahogany casket – the new, more refined term for a coffin – with silver-plated hard-ware and a silk-draped interior.

By the late 19th century, caring for the dead had become a business. Casket-makers such as the Stein Manufacturing Company of Rochester, New York, offered a variety of styles to an increasingly prosperous middle-class public. Embalming, which was now also extolled as a public-health measure, could not be discreetly performed in the home of the deceased. It required special facilities, and this, along with the growth of cities, occupational mobility, and a consequent trend towards smaller dwellings, led to the development of the funeral home. Undertakers – who had come to prefer the more dignified term 'funeral directors' – banded together in 1882 to create the National Funeral Directors' Association. The aim of this brotherhood – virtually all were men – was to elevate their status to that of a profession, by setting educational standards, regulating admission and controlling prices. On the basis of a perceived similarity between embalming and surgery, they sought favourable comparison with both the medical profession and, given the solemnity of their calling, the clergy.

Funeral directors never wholly succeeded in their quest for professional status, but they did become, for the most part, respected members of their communities. They tended to be active in civic affairs, a visibility that accrued directly to the benefit of their funeral homes' call rates. Once established in a community, a well-managed funeral home provided a handsome and dependable income, immune to the economic fluctuations and business cycles that afflict most other areas of commerce. Death rates are highly predictable. There is always a steady supply of corpses, and an equally steady demand for their disposal.

For these reasons, sons routinely followed fathers into the family business. Today, there are about 22,000 funeral homes across the United States; 87 per cent of them are family-owned and have been in the same family for an average of 60 years. By the late 1960s, however, Ray Loewen was beginning to notice a subtle shift in the pattern of funeral-home ownership. It seemed to him – and to others in the business as well – that increasing numbers of funeral homes were coming up for sale, that the offspring of many owners were electing not to stay in the family business. The reasons for this trend, which would accelerate in the coming years, were not, in retrospect, all that difficult to adduce. It was a time of social and political upheaval, with protest marches against the war in Vietnam, and for civil rights in the South. Adolescents were rebelling against the settled ways of their parents. Church attendance was plummeting. And, most pointedly, the funeral trade had come under attack with the publication in 1963 of *The American Way of Death* by Jessica Mitford. The book, which became a bestseller, exposed the secrets of a secretive trade and revealed a contradiction – an hypocrisy, if you will – that many had already begun to suspect. Behind the undertaker's veil of piety, Mitford wrote, was a clever businessman whose sales techniques seemed designed to prey upon the bereavement and guilt of his customers. The book found a large and receptive audience, and suddenly the idea of following one's father into such a business did not seem so appealing.

Loewen, of course, did not share this view of the funeral trade, but he saw opportunity in its development. He began buying funeral homes from owners who had, as he liked to call it, 'succession needs'. He was not the first to do so. In Houston, Robert L. Waltripp, funeral director at a family-run home, had also begun making acquisitions. Waltripp acquired a large home in Winnipeg in

1969, 60 miles from where Loewen had grown up, and he was negotiating for another in Vancouver. Watching Waltripp's rapid growth, Loewen thought he could do something similar. By the end of 1984, he owned 20 additional businesses. The following year, he bought one of the largest and oldest funeral homes in the Canadian Maritimes, J. A. Snow in Halifax, Nova Scotia, which in 1912 had embalmed 300 bodies from the *Titanic* disaster.

Loewen and his chief financial officer, Robert Lundgren, pursued one deal after another. Minutes after they heard word that a funeral home was on the market, they would head for the airport. In Manitoba one night, they closed a deal at four in the morning and, hours later, boarded a plane in pursuit of another deal.

By 1987, Loewen owned 68 funeral homes. All of them were in Canada. Although the United States market was immense and had great potential for consolidation, he knew that many Canadian firms had met a dismal fate in the United States. 'A lot of them get eaten alive,' Lundgren said recently, recalling a discussion that he and Loewen had had on the subject. 'It's very competitive, a very different atmosphere from Canada.'

Nevertheless, that year Loewen found himself presented with two American opportunities that he could not ignore. The first came from a very large funeral home – 1,200 calls – in Flint, Michigan. Still wary of the United

States, he and Lundgren went to Michigan, where they spent considerable time pondering the deal. Before they had a chance to act on it, Loewen got another inquiry, from Fresno, California, from the owner of eight funeral homes known as the Whitehurst Group. This man, who was in his seventies, was ill, and was being courted by an American funeral-home consolidator called Service Corporation International. On meeting him, Loewen recalls that the man vowed to burn his funeral homes to the ground before selling out to Service Corporation International. It seemed to Loewen that destiny had resolved all his doubts about entering the United States market.

Loewen retained the name of every funeral home he acquired and, with it, the base of customers and the goodwill that its former owner had built up in the community. The Loewen name and corporate logo never appeared above a new acquisition's door or on its stationery. Most citizens remained unaware of any change in ownership. This illusion was further abetted by the fact that Loewen, out of necessity as well as inclination, tried to keep many of his acquisitions' key personnel, including the former owners, who tended to stay on to manage day-to-day affairs.

Loewen never regarded this as deception. A successful funeral home's most valuable asset was its reputation in the community, achieved by years of service. And reputation was an asset easily quantified: it was measured by the number of calls a home performed year after year.

Virtually all of Loewen's new acquisitions had turned a profit before he bought them, and he made them even more profitable. Consolidation resulted in efficiencies of scale that were not available to family-owned businesses. Loewen, for example, needed a large supply of coffins. He could bargain with the biggest casket-maker in North America, the Batesville Casket Company of Indiana, for a substantial reduction in price based on volume. The same was true of all the other supplies – from embalming fluids to hearses – needed to operate a funeral home. He made further savings by instituting a centralised accounting system, thereby reducing payroll costs in each home.

Loewen did not pass these savings on to the consumer. He needed the increased margin of profit to pay for the capital costs of acquisition. It was his practice to raise prices immediately by as much as 15 per cent in every newly-acquired funeral home. He called these price increases 'revenue enhancement'. In the funeral business, raising prices traditionally meets with little consumer resistance, at least in the short-term. Most people, in their moment of grief over the death of a family member, do not comparison-shop for funeral services. And most also dislike scrimping – or, at least, to appear to be scrimping –

when it comes to selecting caskets and other burial finery for a loved one.

The Loewen Group, as Loewen now called his company, grew steadily after entering the United States. Loewen acquired 30 or so funeral homes in each of the first three years. Then, in 1990, he doubled the size of his company when, in that single year, he bought 137 funeral homes. The following year, he added 97 more.

Loewen, of course, no longer had time to negotiate the fine contractual details of each new acquisition. He often left that task to a growing staff of experts. He would, however, invariably court the owners of potential new acquisitions. He would invite them up to Vancouver, where he had built a new corporate headquarters. He'd take them out for a cruise up the Canadian coast on his ocean-going yacht, the *Alula Spirit*. The yacht, of the Queenship class, was 110 feet long, required a full-time crew, and had room for cocktail parties of 60 or more people. It became a fixture in Loewen's way of doing business.

In almost every aspect of his personality, Loewen seemed perfectly equipped to sell himself and his company to owners of small funeral homes. As the chief executive of a growing company, he was extroverted, unabashedly garrulous, dictatorial, sometimes quick to anger, and capable of a certain charm when the occasion called for it. When he was not overwhelmed by the pressures of his business, he could only marvel at his own good fortune. He had become a very wealthy man, and the future seemed bright beyond all expectation.

The Loewen Group predicted a 60 per cent increase in death rates in the coming decades, a consequence of the ageing of the postwar baby-boom population. And the potential for funeral-home consolidation in the USA appeared virtually unlimited. His forebodings about doing business in America had proved baseless, like a child's fear of the dark. He surveyed an American landscape of thousands of funeral homes, most of them mom-and-pops (as the consolidators called the family-owned homes), many of them with succession problems of one sort or another looming in the future.

But that was before he ventured into the Deep South. In January 1990, Loewen bought his first funeral home in Mississippi, owned by Robert Riemann in Gulfport. Then he acquired Wright & Ferguson, the largest and most esteemed funeral home in Jackson. Looking back on it some years later, Loewen must have felt that he had unwittingly crossed a border and entered a foreign land, with strange and unpredictable customs. With the purchase of Wright & Ferguson, he set in motion a chain of events, foreseeable to none, that would prove nearly fatal to his company.

The Case

Willie Gary's success has led to extraordinary demands on his time. His secretary receives as many as 75 calls a day from people who insist on talking to him. Many of these calls come from colleges, law schools, bar associations, churches and philanthropic organisations seeking him as a speaker. Some come from lawyers pleading for his assistance in their cases.

On a Wednesday in early May 1995, two lawyers from Mississippi came to Stuart, expecting an audience with Gary. On arriving, they were informed by Gary's secretary that he was working on a case in North Carolina, but that he would return that evening. The two Mississippi lawyers made themselves at home in Gary's reception room, which is as spacious as a hotel lobby, furnished with comfortable sofas and wing chairs.

One of the lawyers, Halbert Dockins, Jr., had met Gary briefly some years earlier at a convention of the Magnolia Bar Association, a group of black lawyers who practise in Mississippi. Gary had been the featured speaker at the convention, and after his speech Dockins, along with many other lawyers, had approached him. Dockins had managed to shake Gary's hand and tell him that he was a source of inspiration. This was manifestly true. Dockins kept on his desk a photograph of Gary seated in his ornately decorated Stuart office. 'When I got depressed,' Dockins once recalled, 'I'd say to myself, "This guy came from nothing. If he can do it, I can do it." '

The lawyer travelling with Dockins was named Michael Cavanaugh. He was white. He and Dockins were not law partners, but they shared a particular client, a Biloxi businessman named Jeremiah O'Keefe. It was on O'Keefe's behalf that they had come to Florida to see Gary.

Dockins and Cavanaugh bided their time in the reception room. Late in the afternoon, Gary's secretary informed them that he would not be returning until Friday. He had asked her to convey his regrets at the delay.

On leaving the reception room, Dockins said to Cavanaugh, 'I'm not going back to Mississippi without talking to him.' They checked into a hotel in Stuart. Cavanaugh spent the next day sunning himself by the pool. Dockins worked out in the exercise room. They ate dinner together. They discussed their client's case. They refined once again the presentation they hoped to make to Gary.

On Friday, they resumed their vigil. When Gary walked into his office at five o'clock that afternoon, Dockins jumped nervously to his feet. Gary grinned broadly at him and embraced him in a hug of the sort that most men reserve for their oldest and best friends, and then only after an absence of years. 'What've you got for me?' Gary asked Dockins. 'You got a PI case for me?'

'Yeah, it's a personal-injury case,' replied Dockins. 'Except it's got a little twist to it.'

In fact, the case had nothing to do with personal injury. It was at heart a commercial case – a contract dispute – and Dockins knew that Gary did not take commercial cases. He felt he needed time to sell the case to Gary. And, besides, in Dockins's mind the injury suffered by his client Jeremiah O'Keefe was indeed personal.

Dockins and Cavanaugh spent several hours with Gary that evening. They described the case to him in broad outline. Their client was a small businessman, the owner of eight funeral parlours in Mississippi and a funeral-insurance business. As clients went, O'Keefe was of the sort a lawyer might dream about. He and his wife, who were now in their early seventies, had 13 children, several of whom worked in the family business. He had served in the state legislature and, for eight years, as mayor of Biloxi. Dockins, seeking every advantage in wooing Gary, added that in 1976 Mayor O'Keefe had refused the Ku-Klux Klan a permit to parade through Biloxi, and that the Klan had spray-painted the words 'nigger lover' on the front door of City Hall.

O'Keefe had built a prosperous business from modest beginnings. The family had been in the funeral trade since the end of the Civil War, when Jeremiah's great-grandfather, the proprietor of a livery service, started hauling coffins. But now, according to Dockins and Cavanaugh, O'Keefe found himself at the mercy of a 'ruthless' and 'predatory' Canadian corporation. That corporation, the Loewen Group, had acquired hundreds of funeral homes across the United States in the past decade. One of its recent acquisitions was in Jackson, Mississippi. O'Keefe had a business relationship of 16 years' duration with the Jackson funeral home. By contract, twice renewed and affirmed, O'Keefe possessed the exclusive right to sell burial insurance for the Jackson funeral home. But, according to O'Keefe, the Loewen Group had refused to honour that contract and had begun selling its own insurance. O'Keefe complained, and filed a lawsuit. Sometime later, he got a call from Ray Loewen, who invited him up to Vancouver to settle their differences. O'Keefe accepted the invitation. He even went for a dinner cruise on Loewen's yacht.

But when O'Keefe returned to Mississippi he found that the Loewen Group was still selling insurance. He renewed his complaint, and got a call from one of Loewen's senior executives. In the months that followed, O'Keefe and the senior executive negotiated a settlement agreement. The agreement called for O'Keefe to sell three funeral homes to Loewen, at a price to be agreed upon, and for Loewen to turn over his Mississippi insurance business to O'Keefe. This agreement seemed to serve the interests of both parties. Loewen wanted funeral homes, and O'Keefe wanted insurance assets. His funeral-insurance company had made a bad investment in a savings-and-loan venture. He needed to supplement his company's cash reserves to meet the requirements of the Mississippi insurance regulators.

O'Keefe signed the agreement, and Loewen's board of directors approved it. Then, according to Dockins and Cavanaugh, Loewen refused to execute the agreement's provisions. They told Gary that O'Keefe had made several concessions in an effort to complete the deal in a timely fashion. More months passed, and more meetings occurred. The Mississippi Insurance Department placed O'Keefe's company under 'administrative supervision'. O'Keefe faced the prospect of losing control of the company that he had worked his whole life to build. To raise cash, he was forced to sell four funeral homes – including the three he had agreed initially to sell to Loewen – to another consolidator, one of Loewen's competitors.

O'Keefe came to the conclusion that Loewen had never intended to complete the deal. He believed that it had been little more than a ruse. If he were to go bankrupt, Loewen could pick up the pieces of his funeral business for a fraction of their real value. O'Keefe amended his original lawsuit. He added a second breach of contract, alleging that the Loewen Group had acted 'fraudulently and maliciously' and had 'breached good faith'. He also asserted that Loewen engaged in 'predatory trade practices' and attempted to create monopolies.

Gary listened patiently throughout this presentation, asking questions now and then. Cavanaugh had the impression that the case did not engage his interest, that he was merely being polite. But Dockins felt encouraged. 'He was so gracious, so courteous,' Dockins recalled later. That evening, Gary invited Dockins and Cavanaugh over to his home on Sewall's Point. He introduced them to his wife and gave them a tour of the palatial villa. In Gary's vast closet, Dockins fingered silky materials and expressed awe. Gary invited Dockins to try on whatever appealed to him, and Dockins did so with relish. Cavanaugh, himself no stranger to the things that money could buy, was also impressed, not so much by Gary's opulence but by his manner.

'He showed us his big house, his automobiles,' Cavanaugh recalls, 'but not in a braggadocio way. He told us he dropped out of school at 14.'

They met again on Saturday morning, in Gary's office. This time, Gary asked one of his partners, Robert Parenti, to sit in on the meeting. He said to Dockins, 'OK, Hal, explain the case to Bob.' Dockins began doing so, with Cavanaugh adding the details.

Dockins had spent many months working on the case. It was a dense thicket of legal theories – predatory trade practices, monopolies and the law of contracts – with which he'd had little experience. He would sit at the counsel table during the trial, but the lead lawyer for O'Keefe, the attorney who would make the opening and closing statements and examine most of the witnesses, was a man named Michael Allred. It was Allred, actually, who had come up with the multiplicity of legal theories that adorned an otherwise straightforward contract case.

At one point, as Dockins laboured to explain the complexities of the case, Gary suddenly jumped up, fists clenched like a boxer ready to deliver body-blows. 'Loewen lied to Jerry O'Keefe!' he shouted. 'He flat-out lied to him!' Dockins was startled by the way Gary brushed aside all the arcane theories and reduced the case to its simplest elements.

'This case,' Gary exclaimed, standing before Dockins and Cavanaugh, his voice raised, 'is about lying, cheating and stealing!'

Dockins and Cavanaugh returned to Mississippi fully convinced that they needed Gary to lead their trial team. But Gary had rejected their pleas to sign on with them. He had told them that he liked the case and he would offer them 'pointers' now and then, but that he simply had too much else to do.

When Jeremiah O'Keefe heard Dockins and Cavanaugh's report, he prepared to embark on his own pilgrimage to see Willie Gary. 'I'll have to take Allred with me,' he told Dockins and Cavanaugh.

'My God,' Dockins exclaimed.

'Don't do it!' Cavanaugh warned.

Michael Allred was intelligent and industrious, and he had an intimate knowledge of the factual minutiae in the case, but he also had a temperament that seemed to create offence wherever he went. He was a large man with ginger hair and a ginger beard, and a stentorian voice. His grandfather had been a member of the Ku-Klux Klan, and Allred had grown up on a farm in the most unregenerate and racist region of Mississippi. He'd even been known to state, in his manner of blunt candour, that he harboured racist attitudes. To many who encountered him, Allred always seemed to be lecturing, instructing and remonstrating, in a tone at once pompous and condescending.

These qualities were not necessarily bad ones in a trial lawyer cross-examining a hostile witness, but they tended to cause problems in everyday life. Dockins, for one, could barely tolerate Allred's presence, and Cavanaugh didn't feel much affection for him either. Even worse, however, was the change that would come over the presiding judge in the case, James E. Graves Jr., a black man, whenever Allred stood before the bench to address him in the pre-trial proceedings. The judge's brow would knit, his eyes would narrow, and his comments would grow more caustic the longer Allred talked. Allred knew that others reacted to him in a prickly fashion, but he attributed this to the fact that he did not, in his words, 'tolerate fools easily'. To Allred, the world was populated largely by fools.

Dockins and Cavanaugh, however, were concerned about the fact that the jury pool in Hinds County, which encompassed the city of Jackson, was approximately two-thirds black. A jury of 12 would, it was most likely, consist of at least six, and perhaps as many as eight or nine, black citizens. To have Allred addressing such a jury, in front of a judge who did not like him, seemed risky indeed.

There were other reasons for concern. A month earlier, the Loewen Group, which was already employing a large corporate-law firm in Jackson, and another one in Chicago, just to oversee the case, had added two black lawyers to its legal team. One of these lawyers was an elected state senator, the other a state representative and chairman of the black Congressional caucus. Both of the lawyers were able, but it was not as if Loewen needed additional able lawyers. 'They were already wheeling briefs in on dollies,' Dockins recalled. He viewed the arrival of the new lawyers as racial pandering of the most blatant sort. 'We've been out-blacked,' he told O'Keefe. 'Loewen is stacking the deck with black politicians.' Dockins had contended that they needed to counter Loewen's moves with a first-class trial lawyer, and he had one in mind – one who, as fortune would have it, happened to be black.

Despite Dockins's and Cavanaugh's fears about Allred, O'Keefe brought him to the meeting with Gary, but he took the precaution of preceding Allred by 24 hours, so that he could speak to Gary alone.

They met for the first time at the Indian River Plantation, where O'Keefe had booked rooms, a short drive from Gary's office. Over dinner, each man took the measure of the other. They were, in every physical aspect, a study in contrasts.

O'Keefe had a ruddy complexion, pale-blue eyes, and hair as white as a lawyer's starched shirt. He stood an inch over six feet, but even at the age of 72 his erect carriage and robust frame made him appear taller. He possessed the sombre dignity of a funeral director, but his manner was also inflected with humour and warmth. This, at least, was what Gary saw in O'Keefe.

'I flat-out liked him,' Gary recalled later. 'Some clients will tell you what they think you need to hear to take a case. He didn't do that. And my wife fell in love with the guy. She said, "You've got to help him."'

The next afternoon, O'Keefe went to pick up Allred at the Palm Beach airport. He lectured him at length on how he should comport himself with Gary, the new lead counsel. Allred appeared to take his change in status in his stride. And, indeed, in a meeting that afternoon Allred ceded control of the case to Gary with a measure of grace. They engaged in lively discussion about the details of the case. It wasn't until the next morning, when Allred was clearly feeling relaxed in Gary's company, that he announced, 'There's something you should know about me, Willie.'

Gary looked up.

'I am prejudiced,' Allred said. 'But I'm trying to work on it. It's sort of like when an alcoholic goes to Alcoholics Anonymous.'

Gary's eyes opened fractionally wider. Then he nodded and said, 'That's a very good thing to be working on, Mike.'

Gary announced his presence on the legal team to the Loewen Group in June, three months before the start of the trial, by dispatching a settlement demand. Just six months earlier, in January, Cavanaugh and Dockins had tried to settle the case at a meeting in Cincinnati with Loewen Group executives and lawyers. Cavanaugh had started by asking for $6.5 million. He recalls that Loewen's lawyers reacted with incredulity, and then with derision. By the end of the meeting, Cavanaugh remembers, 'I did everything but get down on my knees and beg for four million. They said, "That's outrageous! Our client would fire us if we brought that back to him."'

Gary now proposed a different amount, a sum he had arrived at with the help of Allred. O'Keefe's actual financial damages, according to Allred, came to about $16 million. This was a figure that even a dispassionate observer might have regarded as inflated, but Allred also had his eyes on punitive damages, which a jury may award, if it sees fit, to punish especially bad acts. In Gary's view, the cost to Loewen for settling the entire case should be $125 million, a demand almost 20 times greater than the offer that the Loewen Group had summarily rejected in January.

Loewen and his lawyers ignored the new settlement demand. For O'Keefe, the only indication that Loewen had even received the demand occurred when Loewen hired another lawyer. This lawyer, whose name was Richard Sinkfield, came from Atlanta. He was an experienced trial lawyer. He specialised in anti-trust law and complex business litigation. And he was also black.

The Trial

On the morning of 12 September 1995, when Willie Gary introduced Jeremiah O'Keefe to the pool of prospective jurors in the matter of *O'Keefe* v *The Loewen Group, Inc.*, he made a point of walking over to the counsel table and putting his hand on his client's shoulder. Throughout the day of jury selection and the next day, during his opening statement, whenever he mentioned O'Keefe's name he would generally return to the counsel table and put his hand on O'Keefe's shoulder. Often during the next two months, until the day in November when the jury returned its verdict, he continued this ritual. He did not, of course, do it every single time – not in the heat of his cross-examination of Ray Loewen, for example – but he did it so frequently and with such deliberate intent that the jury of 12 citizens (eight of whom were black) could not escape taking note.

At the counsel table, sitting beside O'Keefe throughout the trial, was his wife of 50 years, Annette, who was plump and diminutive. Behind them, occupying the first row of the gallery, were at least six and sometimes as many as ten of their 13 grown-up children. This family tableau – the elderly, dignified undertaker and his wife, their good and handsome children – had been assembled and framed by Gary for the edification of the jury. For good measure, he also had on display an actual photograph, greatly enlarged, of the extended O'Keefe family.

The purpose of all this was not lost on the lawyers representing Loewen. They could do nothing about the presence of the O'Keefe family in the courtroom, but on the first morning of the trial they did object strenuously to the photograph.

The issue in dispute, Richard Sinkfield told the judge, concerned a contract, not the familial warmth of the O'Keefe family: 'The only purpose for which this kind of exhibition is being offered is to try to incur sympathy and favour out of the jury.'

Sinkfield was, of course, absolutely right. Gary made it apparent from the outset that he intended to cast the trial as a morality play – a case about 'the oldest sin known to anybody, and that's greed'. O'Keefe's role in this drama was that of a man of honour and principle, a man of 'family values' who 'would fight for what's right and what he believes in'. Playing opposite O'Keefe, in the role of the villain, was the foreigner from Canada, Ray Loewen: 'A man,' Gary told the jury, 'who wouldn't keep his word, deceived people, and would not deal with honour,' a man who sought to 'dominate markets, create monopolies and gouge families that are grieving.'

Ray Loewen played the role of villain in absentia, for the most part. He was busy running his company, acquiring more funeral homes, and negotiating with banks for credit to finance those acquisitions. 'I didn't think I needed to go to Jackson for the trial,' Loewen said later. 'This was completely off the radar screen for me.' He knew about Gary's settlement demand of $125 million, but he regarded it as a ridiculous, perhaps desperate, ploy. His legal counsel had assured him that he would win the case. And even if, for some unforeseen reason, he did not win, the maximum probable exposure his company faced, his lawyers told him, would be a loss of between $6 million and $12 million, the approximate amount of O'Keefe's damages.

Five lawyers sat at the Loewen counsel table. More Loewen lawyers watched the proceedings from the gallery. Some of them had never worked together before. More than once, Judge Graves noticed a Loewen lawyer at the counsel table looking with incredulity – 'as if to say, "What the hell is he doing?"' – at another Loewen lawyer examining a witness.

'Demeanour is important from the moment you walk into the courtroom,' the judge later remarked. 'And the jurors noticed everything.'

Their feelings about each other aside, Loewen's lawyers remained unshaken in their belief that they would prevail on the merits of the case. They might grudgingly agree that Gary had, from time to time, put on a good show, but in their reports to Loewen they insisted that he had not touched them on the only issue that really mattered – the execution of the contracts. They took delight in Judge Graves's thinly concealed dislike for Allred, certain that the jurors saw it too. Every argument won at a bench conference, every objection sustained, affirmed their belief that they were destined to win. Arguments lost and objections overruled were usually deemed inconsequential or, at worst, excellent grounds for appeal, in the unlikely event that it should come to that.

There was no dispute about the fact that O'Keefe had a valid contract of 16 years' duration with the Wright & Ferguson funeral home to sell burial insurance. Nor was there any doubt that O'Keefe and the Loewen Group had negotiated and signed an agreement, which was meant to resolve Loewen's alleged breach of the Wright & Ferguson contract. Loewen's lawyers claimed that he had never breached the contract, but this proved a difficult claim to defend. 'Didn't breach the contract?' Gary asked at one point during the trial. 'Well, why did you come down here to Mississippi to sign a settlement agreement? You don't go making settlements if you haven't breached a contract.'

And then, according to Gary, the signed agreement – itself a contract – was also breached. Loewen's lawyers acknowledged that the provisions of the settlement had never been executed, but they claimed that the document was really more of an 'agreement to agree' than a binding contract, and that in the end the parties simply could not come to an agreement. Gary had another explanation for the jury: 'They wanted Jerry out of business. They used that settlement agreement to dangle in front of him. They started coming up with all these excuses, one after another, one after another, one after another, and, poor man, he made one concession after another. They beat him down, 72 years old, they beat him down, they beat him and they beat him, and it's not right!'

Gary wanted the jury to see a pattern in the fact that Loewen had violated not just one but two contracts, and argued that Loewen's method of doing business infected his entire operation. By way of illustration, Gary's team offered the town of Corinth, Mississippi, where Loewen owned all three funeral homes that catered to the white population.

Among the array of coffins and burial wares sold by these funeral homes was an item called the Wilbert Copper Triune Vault, manufactured by the Wilbert Burial Vault Company. The container was a two-ton box with a concrete exterior and a copper lining – a feature that, according to the sales literature, made the vault watertight. These concrete boxes lacked the aesthetic appeal of the caskets they would contain – of the Aurora 'Brushed Blue Pietà,' for example, or the Batesville 'Emerald Mist' – but they provided customers with additional 'peace of mind' in laying their loved ones to rest. Wilbert sold the Copper Triune to funeral homes for $940, a sum that included the cost of shipping. The funeral homes were free to charge their customers whatever they saw fit, and it was standard practice among most to double the price. But in the town of Corinth, where Loewen had almost no competition, the price to consumers was $2,860, more than triple the wholesale cost.

Two hundred miles away, in Jackson, where Loewen had more competition, his Wright & Ferguson funeral home sold the Copper Triune for $1,920, about the same price as his competitors. 'Some poor fellow has to pay a thousand dollars more for just a box? Just a box!' exclaimed Gary. 'They are just shipped out by the people who make them. Funeral home doesn't even have to touch it, doesn't have to put it in the hearse, doesn't have to shovel one bit of dirt. They charge $2,860, that's almost $2,000 for making the phone call! That ain't right! Talking about a monopoly, deceptive trade practices!'

As further proof of Loewen's desire to monopolise the funeral market, Gary's team put to repeated use a memo from Loewen's own files, written by a senior executive named Don Holmstrom. 'We would be able to beat O'Keefe to that [Jackson] market by at least six months,' Holmstrom had written. 'In addition, with the strength of the Wright/Ferguson and Baldwin Lee names, I believe we would easily dominate the market.'

This is the sort of language that might be found in the files of any company assessing its strength and opportunity in a given market. Indeed, when Holmstrom was confronted on the witness stand with his memo, and with the phrase 'dominate the market', he said, 'I think that's the goal of every business person.' But the language took on a sinister hue as Gary summoned one witness after another to attest to the Loewen Group's putative greed. There was Lorraine McGrath, a former comptroller for Loewen in the Mississippi region, who had worked on various acquisitions, including the purchase of the Corinth funeral homes. She had quit her job, she testified, in large part because of a crisis of conscience.

'The Loewen Group had a consistent policy at that time of raising prices on a fairly regular basis,' she stated. 'And I was not sure any longer that I agreed with that. It was a personal decision that at some point we should say, "The price is high enough." '

John Wright, the former president of Wright & Ferguson and for five years a member of Loewen's board of directors, was called to testify on Loewen's behalf. In this instance, it was Dockins who conducted the cross-examination. He succeeded in turning Wright into a witness against Loewen. 'Of the 300 acquisitions that

Loewen has made since you've been on the board,' Dockins said to Wright, 'have you ever known him not to raise prices once he got those companies?'

'I don't know of a case where he did not raise prices,' Wright admitted. 'But then I did not have any knowledge of how the businesses were being operated when he took them over.'

'Isn't it true,' Dockins asked, 'that after he acquired the Wright & Ferguson Funeral Home, he raised prices on all of your customers?'

'Yes, prices were raised after we sold.'

'Did he consult you about raising prices on your customers all these years before he did it?'

'No,' Wright said, 'we had no discussion.'

***

Ray Loewen arrived in Jackson in mid-October. He brought his wife, Anne, with him. At Jackson airport, the Loewen corporate jet was parked right next to Gary's jet. From his plane Loewen read the words 'Wings of Justice' emblazoned along the fuselage of Gary's plane.

Loewen smiled cheerfully on his first morning in the courtroom and shook hands with everyone in reach. He made a point of walking over to the O'Keefe family members and delivering a warm greeting to Annette O'Keefe, who looked a little stunned but managed a smile of her own and a civil reply. He sat at the counsel table with his lawyers and listened to testimony. He had no first-hand experience of the American civil-justice system. In Canada, a case such as this would have been tried in front of a judge, not a jury of laymen who knew nothing about the law of contracts.

By the end of the first morning, Loewen's demeanour had undergone a radical change. He had taken the temperature of the courtroom, and he did not like the results. His affable manner turned brusque. At the noon recess, he summoned his lawyers into a conference room across from the courtroom. Members of the O'Keefe family reported hearing an angry voice coming from the conference room. 'He was chewing butt,' one of the O'Keefe children said.

Some days later, Loewen took the witness stand in his own defence. Guided by Sinkfield, he spoke with pride about his company, the hard work he had invested in it, and the cordial relations he kept with the owners of the funeral homes he had acquired. 'We're known for our dinner cruises,' he told the jury. 'We love to entertain funeral directors from across America. They come up in the late afternoon usually, and it's a very pleasant way of establishing relationships, having dinner on our boat.'

He recalled few actual details of his dealings with O'Keefe, although he did remember the time O'Keefe and Allred came to Vancouver to discuss the Wright & Ferguson contract. 'We had a very pleasant dinner cruise on our boat at that time.'

He had no recollection of ever saying to O'Keefe that he 'didn't object to settling disputes in court'. His intentions all along, he insisted, had been honourable. The failure to complete the agreement had resulted from a difference in the valuation of O'Keefe's properties, not from deceit or bad faith.

The subject of Loewen's boat had come up several times during the trial. Gary had been the first to mention it, six weeks earlier, in his opening statement – 'A yacht that the company allows him to spend a million dollars a year just to keep,' he'd said – and with that single, off-hand remark Loewen's lawyers had felt compelled to defend the boat. They did so at great length. One Loewen executive, under a friendly examination by a Loewen lawyer, testified that the company did not actually own a boat. 'From time to time, we rent a boat.'

'Who owns the boat that you rent?' the lawyer asked.

'The boat is owned by a private company, which, in turn, is owned by Mr Raymond Loewen. We rent it on a daily basis. To ensure that it's available on short notice, we pay what's called a standby fee.'

And on it went, with a thorough description of how useful the boat was for doing business, and the manner in which the board of directors set the rental rate. At a bench conference with the lawyers the next morning, Judge Graves warned against any more boat talk.

'They spent a whole hour yesterday trying to explain that we don't have a big yacht, but we do,' the judge said. 'I'm so sick of hearing about that. I'm the only person in here without a boat, and I've got to hear about these dinner cruises.'

But it didn't end there. With Loewen on the witness stand, Sinkfield resumed the subject for reasons no one – not even Loewen, apparently – could fathom. 'You mentioned dinner cruises,' said Sinkfield. 'Is that a boat or is that a yacht?'

'I really don't know the difference,' Loewen replied.

'It's a big boat, isn't it?' Sinkfield asked.

'I don't know what's big, but it is 110 feet long. I'm not sure if that is big.'

That was all Gary needed to begin his cross-examination.

'Let me ask you this,' he said to Loewen. 'Does your board of directors know that you don't know the difference between a boat and a yacht?'

'I've had the privilege of entertaining my directors on my boat,' Loewen replied.

'Do they know that you don't know the difference between a boat and a yacht?'

'I doubt if they know that,' Loewen said.

'Can you land a helicopter on your canoe, boat, or yacht, whichever one?'

'My helicopter pilot can land a helicopter on my boat.'

'Oh,' Gary said, 'you've got your own helicopter and your own pilot?'

Three days later, in closing arguments, Gary told the jury, 'These people just lied, lied, lied, lied. They lied to Jerry and they lied to you. They even lied for no reason. They lie. What about the boat? Nothing wrong with the man having a yacht, but, if you've got a yacht, say it!'

He assembled the evidence of the previous two months into a story that appeared almost seamless in its contours and particulars. It helped that the facts – most of them, anyhow – supported the story. The single weak link – the terms of the contract between O'Keefe and Wright & Ferguson, and whether Loewen had actually violated these terms – he brushed effortlessly aside.

'You can go with a whole lot of fancy stuff,' he said to the jury. 'And I told you that I was just a country boy and I said I might not use big fancy words like everybody else. You said you wouldn't hold that against me because I wanted to talk common to you. The bottom line is they broke their word. They broke their word, and it was intentional and it was malicious.'

And, of course, he also told the jury, that Loewen also

dominated markets, created monopolies, and, worst of all, gouged grieving families. 'If you really want to gouge someone, you catch them during that time when they've lost a mother or a father or a child. They are helpless. They are helpless. They are there for the picking. Take them, take them. It's all about dollars with them.'

After enumerating these sins, Gary methodically enumerated the sums of money that Loewen should pay to O'Keefe for the damages he had inflicted. There were many categories, all attested to by experts in economics and in the funeral business, and in the end it added up to $125 million. And then, almost as an afterthought, Gary said to the jury, 'You may think that is not enough.'

It was late on Friday afternoon by the time the lawyers had finished their final arguments, so the jury did not begin deliberating until the following Monday morning at eight o'clock. To reach a verdict, only nine of the 12 jurors had to come to an agreement. Given the length of the trial, the complexity of Judge Graves's instructions on the law, and, especially, the nine-page interrogatory that the jurors had to answer in order to return a verdict, everyone presumed that the jury would take days to arrive at a decision.

On commencing their deliberations, the jurors selected a 63-year-old white man named Glenn Millen as their foreman. He was well-educated, an electrical engineer by training, and, although he had lived for the past 30 years in the United States, he was Canadian by birth. He had once served as a juror in a civil case in which the jury had found for the defendant. All in all, he appeared to be the embodiment of the perfect juror for Loewen.

Loewen's lawyers had remained steadfast in the belief that they would prevail on the legal merits of the case, until the moment on Wednesday afternoon when the bailiff passed the verdict slip to the judge. Some of Loewen's team had derided Gary's final argument as 'undisciplined and demagogic', a 'stream-of-consciousness' rant. The Jackson lawyer who had worked on the case for Loewen since its inception, almost four years earlier, brought his children to the courtroom to witness the announcement of the verdict. Loewen and his wife sat together at the counsel table for the rendering of the verdict. 'My senior counsel were telling me that we were ahead on the merits, and I could not believe that we wouldn't win on the merits,' Loewen recalls. 'The defence team,' Judge Graves remarked later, 'never had any idea how out of touch they were with what was going on.'

O'Keefe and his wife sat opposite Loewen at the plaintiff's counsel table with their lawyers. O'Keefe had instructed his family not to utter a word in the courtroom, whether he won or lost. Cavanaugh had a seat at the end of the counsel table, a vantage point that gave him a direct view of Loewen. In answer to the first question – whether Loewen had breached the Wright & Ferguson contract – Judge Graves read that the jury had said 'Yes' and had awarded O'Keefe $31.2 million in compensatory damages.

Cavanaugh saw Loewen turn suddenly pale. There were ten questions in all, and each one was answered in the affirmative, followed by a large sum of money. It took the judge almost ten minutes to read the verdict slip in its entirety. By the end, Cavanaugh saw that Loewen looked stupefied, with the glazed eyes and the pallor of a man in a near-clinical state of shock. The jury had awarded O'Keefe a total of $260 million.

Indeed, Loewen was in shock. 'I could not believe what I was hearing,' he said of that moment. 'I was absolutely stunned. I thought, "This can't be happening."'

At Sinkfield's request, Judge Graves polled the jurors, and then he explained that they had one more task remaining. The nature of the proceedings required that they return on the following morning to consider the issue of punitive damages, and this meant that there would be a presentation of the Loewen Group's net worth. The judge assured the jurors that the presentation would take only one day.

At the courthouse the next morning, Judge Graves called the lawyers into his chambers and informed them that he had received a note from the jury foreman. The note stated that the jurors had already considered punitive damages in returning their verdict. It had been their intention to award $100 million in compensatory damages and $160 million in punitive damages.

Loewen's lawyers immediately asked for a retrial on the grounds that the verdict was 'contrary to the evidence' and that the foreman's note had made it clear that the jurors had 'completely ignored the instructions of the court'.

'That motion is denied,' the judge replied, and he went on to say that he felt inclined to accept the note as clarification of the jury's award and to let the verdict stand. The parties, of course, had to agree to this. If they did not, he would have to send the jury back to reconsider the verdict.

'This note makes it clear that they're going to award $100 million in compensatory damages,' the judge said. 'If I go back in there, I'm also going to allow the plaintiffs to put on their evidence of the defendant's net worth.'

Gary consulted briefly with his colleagues. They agreed to accept the verdict as it stood, providing Loewen waived any appeal on the failure to present evidence concerning net worth. But Loewen's lawyers refused to make such a deal.

Judge Graves regarded the Loewen legal team with a look of surprise. 'I don't think you want to go back in there,' he said to them. 'You already know they've given $160 million without knowing net worth.'

By now, Gary was having second thoughts of his own. He wanted a clean verdict, one that would survive an appeal by Loewen on procedural grounds, and he also rather liked the idea of talking to this jury one more time. 'Let's try it!' he exclaimed. 'Let's try it!'

When the jurors returned, Gary told them, 'You need to have all the cards on the table. And one of the things you didn't have on the table was how much money these people are worth.'

He called two economists to the witness stand. Both testified that, after an examination of the Loewen Group's annual statements, and forms filed with the Securities and Exchange Commission, they had concluded that the company's net worth exceeded $3 billion. Sinkfield asserted in his presentation to the jury that the Loewen Group had a net worth of only $411 million. But the economist called to testify on Loewen's behalf stated that, in his opinion, the company was worth between $600 million and $700 million.

This was, by any measure, an extraordinary and – for Loewen – grievous example of a poorly co-ordinated presentation by his legal team. But Loewen wasn't there that day to witness it. He had already left town, unable to face the ordeal of sitting once again in the courtroom.

Gary, of course, exploited the error without remorse. 'Members of the jury, they came in here even up to this morning trying to weasel and slip and slide. The net worth of this company went from $411 million to almost $700 million in less than 30 minutes. That's what we've been dealing with.'

He pointed out that Loewen owned nearly 800 funeral homes and 172 cemeteries. 'You think,' he said, in a voice pitching high with incredulity, 'that Ray Loewen would sell all of that business, all of those companies, for $411 million?'

And he did not fail to point out Loewen's absence. 'He didn't even show up today. That's the ultimate arrogance.'

For all of Loewen's sins, Gary asked the jury to award $1 billion in punitive damages. In his ringing and powerful voice – his pulpit voice – he repeatedly uttered the sum with its plosive consonant: 'One billion dollars, one billion dollars, ladies and gentlemen of the jury.'

This time, the jurors' deliberation was brief. In less than an hour, they returned a verdict of $400 million in punitive damages. Along with compensatory damages, the total award came to half a billion dollars. Several of the jurors revealed later that they had been only a single vote short of awarding $1 billion.

The Settlement

The victory party took place at Mary Mahoney's Old French House Restaurant, in Biloxi, the evening after the jury's final award. A huge throng of revellers gathered for the celebration, which went on for many hours, and was interrupted now and then by calls for quiet and speeches by the lawyers. Willie Gary sang *Stand By Me* and dedicated it to Annette O'Keefe, who had fallen ill with heart palpitations in the waning days of the trial. The bill for the evening came to more than $8,000.

On Monday 6 November, Judge Graves signed the formal entry of judgment in the amount of $500 million for the plaintiffs. By then, both parties had begun weighing the consequences of such a staggering verdict. The law of Mississippi required Loewen to post a cash bond of 125 per cent of the judgment – $625 million – if he chose to appeal the verdict. One intent of this law is to prevent litigants who have lost at trial from dissipating their assets during the pendency of an appeal. But for Loewen – indeed, for any company, even a very large one – to post a cash bond of that size was no easy matter.

O'Keefe had no doubt that Loewen would like to appeal if he was able. Neither O'Keefe nor Gary relished the idea of an appeal, which could take years to grind its way through the judicial system, and could also, of course, end in a reversal. The day after the entry of judgment, O'Keefe asked Gary to contact Loewen's lawyers with the aim of settling the case.

The first meeting took place in New Orleans, in a conference room at the Hotel Intercontinental. Gary later said that it was as if Loewen's lawyers were still 'in a coma'. They made an offer of less than $20 million. Angry words were exchanged. They raised the offer to $25 million. 'You act like you just won the case!' Gary exclaimed. 'We got a verdict for five hundred million – and that's what we want.'

By now, Loewen had begun to suspect that he was the victim of a conspiracy. In time, this suspicion grew to an absolute conviction. He could never have adduced the proof to support a conspiracy, yet he saw coincidence and dark synchronicity everywhere. Among other things, he had read a novel by John Grisham called *The Runaway Jury*, about a fictional lawsuit tried in Biloxi, of all places, in which a juror conspires to deliver a huge verdict. The truth about his own case, he came to believe, was a conspiracy that was more twisted than even this fiction. He could not conceive that his circumstances might be the product of his own making, or even just bad luck.

His circumstances were desperate. Even if, by some miracle, he did manage to post the $625 million bond, and avoid immediate bankruptcy, that in itself would have serious repercussions for the company. The premium payments and interest would amount to tens of millions of dollars, and it would affect the warranties and covenants made to banks that had financed the acquisition of several hundred funeral homes. The lines of credit he had established to fuel the growth of his company would dry up.

In public, Loewen kept up his usual optimistic demeanour. 'We were all operating in the belief that the courts couldn't allow anything of that magnitude; that justice would prevail,' one senior executive recalls. 'It was just so grossly absurd. We'd thought we'd get through it – that it was just one of those crazy things.'

Loewen's lawyers, meanwhile, were working feverishly. They filed motions for a new trial, for a reversal of the verdict and entry of judgment on Loewen's behalf, and, of course, for a reduction in the amount of the award. Judge Graves heard oral argument on these motions on 20 November. He later remarked that he believed the verdict for O'Keefe had been a proper one, although he intimated that he would have awarded a much smaller sum if the case had been tried before the bench. He declined none the less to reduce it. That, he believed, was the province of the Mississippi Supreme Court.

After the hearing, Gary said, 'They have ten days to post the cash bond. If they don't, my client will proceed to take over their assets. That's every funeral home they own, every insurance company, every cemetery, their corporate jet, and their yacht.' He had Dockins and Allred preparing lists of Loewen's property and drafting notices of seizure.

Loewen's lawyers issued an immediate appeal to the Supreme Court for relief on the amount of the bond, suggesting instead a bond of $125 million. But on 24 January the Mississippi Supreme Court ruled that Loewen would have to post the entire $625 million by noon on 31 January. Shares in Loewen stock plummeted.

The day after the Supreme Court's ruling, Gary wrote a letter to Loewen's lawyers. 'Please be advised', it stated, 'that as of 12 noon, Wednesday 31 January 1996, we shall start execution on all property, real and personal, that you have in the state of Mississippi and in other states as well.' He offered them a last chance 'to resolve this case and avoid bankruptcy' by means of settlement. He renewed an earlier offer to settle for $475 million.

That same morning, the phones began ringing in Jeremiah O'Keefe's office. Most of the calls came from New York, from brokers and investment houses that had stakes in Loewen stock. O'Keefe finally talked to one of the most persistent callers, an industry analyst from Goldman Sachs.

'You won't settle,' the analyst said angrily, 'and that's unreasonable.'

'That's a lie,' O'Keefe replied, and went on to say that Loewen apparently did not want to settle. He had not attended any settlement discussions, nor had he sent anyone with authority to settle.

'How much money do you want?' the analyst asked.

'I'm not saying how much. There's no offer on the table.'

'I'm calling Loewen right now,' the analyst said.

Later that day, one of the Loewen vice-presidents named Larry Miller called and told O'Keefe that the Loewen Group had authorised him to negotiate a settlement. 'I'm willing to sit down if you are,' Miller said. They agreed to meet at the Ritz-Carlton in Atlanta the next morning at 11 o'clock.

O'Keefe brought Michael Allred with him to Atlanta, where he met Gary and his partners, Lorenzo Williams and Robert Parenti. Miller awaited them in a conference room upstairs with yet another Loewen lawyer, who this time was from San Francisco. In response to Gary's demand for $475 million, Miller offered $50 million.

Gary's response was to tell him, 'I'm going to hire an undertaker and an embalmer and bury y'all.'

Thus began what Miller later called 'a very painful, very long, all-night process', punctuated by frequent tirades and one party or another going off to caucus and regain its composure. By the evening, they had made little progress. The meeting broke up, and each party went out to dinner. Gary asked O'Keefe, 'What would you settle for, Jerry?' Without so much as a pause, O'Keefe said, 'Fifty million; what they've already offered. I'm not leaving here without an agreement.' Gary shook his head sadly, and O'Keefe could tell that he had disappointed him.

Throughout the day, Gary and Allred had done most of the talking. O'Keefe had remained mostly silent. At around 11 o'clock that evening, as Miller recalls it, he turned to O'Keefe and addressed him directly. Miller said, 'Mr O'Keefe, you have to listen to me and keep your advisers quiet for a minute. You have to decide how much money is enough, how much you really need.'

Miller left unsaid the fact that O'Keefe, at 72, would not have many years left to enjoy the fruits of his victory, and he certainly would not choose to spend those years in litigation, or squabbling with other creditors over the bankrupt remains of Loewen.

Miller did not say these things, but everyone in the room understood them. O'Keefe began to speak, and neither Gary nor Allred interrupted him. O'Keefe told Miller he would accept $50 million in cash, one million shares of Loewen stock at a guaranteed price of $30 a share, and a promissory note, payable over 20 years, to the amount of $200 million.

And from this began the final negotiation that would, after more hours of wrangling over structure, guarantees and sums, finally result in a settlement. By four o'clock in the morning, they had a contract to fax to Loewen for his signature. There remained, however, one small item to agree upon.

Loewen refused to sign the contract unless he was given assurance from Gary that he would not represent a litigant in a case against him for the following three years. Loewen offered to pay a retainer of $20,000 per year for this assurance, and Gary agreed.

The Fee

All lawsuits are unique. Most are unique in ways that concern no one but the litigants. They set no new precedents and pose no special legal or intellectual challenges. They occur beneath the threshold of public recognition. In the case of *O'Keefe* v *The Loewen Group Inc.*, however, the sheer size of the verdict and the ensuing settlement made news throughout the United States, in the pages of the *New York Times* and, predictably, on the op-ed page of the *Wall Street Journal*, under the headline 'A Small Canadian Firm Meets The American Tort Monster'.

The award was, of course, outlandish and utterly out of proportion both to the damages and to Jeremiah O'Keefe's expectations. But it was also a rare occurrence, notwithstanding the cries of warning from the *Wall Street Journal*. Until Gary arrived in Mississippi, the largest previous legal award in that state had been $18 million.

Ray Loewen and his company survived the ordeal. Indeed, it appeared for a while that he was prospering. His stock recovered from a post-verdict plunge to the teens and reached a high of $42 per share. In two equity offerings during the year following the verdict, he raised $382 million and acquired over half a billion dollars' worth of funeral homes and cemeteries. He fought off a hostile takeover attempt by his larger and more powerful rival, Service Corporation International. After his near-death experience in Mississippi, he seemed jubilant about the future.

Mississippi, however, was not just a bad memory but a harbinger. In Loewen's zeal for growth – a zeal that some said was fuelled by delusions of wealth, grandeur and power – he grew too fast. He burdened his company with a crushing debt. Two years after the verdict, he reported a loss of almost $600 million. In October 1998, Loewen was forced to resign as president and CEO of his own company. Less than a year later, in June 1999, the Loewen

Group, with its shares trading for 53 cents on the New York Stock Exchange, was declared bankrupt.

Loewen, reportedly, now lives in a condominium in Hawaii. He is regarded as a pariah in the funeral industry; thousands of former funeral-home owners whose property he bought are left with virtually worthless promissory notes and stock. Lawsuits against him and his company have proliferated like mushrooms in a forest.

In the legal papers filed during bankruptcy, Loewen executives claim that the O'Keefe litigation has had 'a lasting, damaging effect on... their overall financial health'. That claim seems extravagant, given the $3.2 billion of debt that the company had amassed. But although Mississippi was not the direct cause of Loewen's woe, it cannot be dismissed altogether. 'Sort of like the *Titanic* popping a rivet,' said one of O'Keefe's sons.

In September 2000, O'Keefe and a group of investors submitted a proposal to the Loewen Group bankruptcy authorities. He offered to buy, at a price of $98 million, all 75 funeral homes and 34 cemeteries (and an insurance company) that Loewen still owned in Mississippi, Alabama and Louisiana. O'Keefe is not unaware of the irony in offering to buy Loewen's property with what was Loewen's money, but he is, above all else, a shrewd businessman who does not like to let a good opportunity slip by.

On the scale of ironic outcomes, the matter of Willie Gary's fee in the Mississippi case is worth noting. The settlement negotiated by O'Keefe and Larry Miller came to $129 million. Gary was entitled to 25 per cent of that sum. He received $12,500,000 of the cash portion of the settlement, and 375,000 shares of stock, as well as his percentage of an $80 million non-interest-bearing note. For his part, O'Keefe sold his share of Loewen's stock when the price reached $38.70. He called Gary and urged him to do the same, but Gary never did. That stock, of course, is now worth practically nothing, and so is the note. O'Keefe believes that Gary was just too busy trying cases to care much about the stock.

O'Keefe feels great affection for Gary. After the trial, they saw each other often, on occasions both formal and informal. When Annette O'Keefe died of heart failure in 1998, aged 74, Gary attended her funeral. It was held, of course, in Biloxi, at the flagship funeral home of the O'Keefe family, and it resembled the sort of funeral that a head of state might receive, attended by 1,000 mourners.

In speeches at churches, colleges and law associations, Gary has often remarked on the fact that he – the great-great-grandson of slaves – represented a man who was the great-grandson of slave-owners. This observation could serve many possible ends, social and political, but Willie Gary seems to intend it only as an illustration of individual initiative, of how the work ethic and the will to succeed can triumph over great adversity.

The reference to slave-owning forebears is the sole thing that Gary has ever said to irk O'Keefe. 'I've told him my family never owned slaves,' O'Keefe says. 'My great-grandfather was a dirt-poor farmer. Willie, he gets kind of carried away sometimes.'

AUTHOR BIOGRAPHY

Jonathan Harr lives and works in Northampton, Massachusetts. His book, A Civil Action, *was awarded the 1995 National Book Critics' Circle Award and made into a major Hollywood film. The rights to this story have been bought by Warner Brothers.*

Other books in the **FRONTLINES** series:

The Strange World of Thomas Harris
Inside the mind of the creator of Hannibal Lecter
David Sexton

British Teeth
An excruciating journey from the dentist's chair to the
rotten heart of a nation
William Leith

Last Drink to to LA
Cleaning up on the West Coast of America:
confessions of an AA survivor
John Sutherland

Your Pedigree Chum
Like most dog-lovers, Missy's owners think she is irreplaceable –
and they are rich enough to do something about it
James Langton

Nurse Wolf & Dr Sacks
This is New York...a dominatrix and
a doctor share tales of the city
Paul Theroux

Also published by Short Books, **Short Lives:**

The Voice of Victorian Sex: Arthur H. Clough
Rupert Christiansen

The Boy Who Inspired Thomas Mann's
'Death in Venice': Wladyslaw Moes
Gilbert Adair

A Material Girl: Bess of Hardwick
Kate Hubbard

Inventor of the Disposable Culture:
King Camp Gillette
Tim Dowling

Last Action Hero of the British Empire:
Cdr John Kerans
Nigel Farndale

The Hungarian Who Walked to Heaven:
Alexander Csoma de Koros
Edward Fox

Discoverer of the Human Heart: William Harvey
Ronan Bennett

The Hated Wife: Carrie Kipling
Adam Nicolson